"The questions in this jou easily change my persp "MAKING MISTAKES IS STRIVING TOWARDS A GOAL" helped me rethink how I can look at the mistakes I have made as helping me towards reaching my goal rather than another setback. I have tried many times in the past to rethink how I look at my mistakes but have not been able to really make any progress until reading this book. I highly recommend this gem of a book!"

—Jodi Bimberg, Story Strategist, *LifeMaven*

"Phyllis has this ability to reach right off the pages and talk to me. Her words are insightful and powerful. I am left with a call to action, producing results."

—Carin Mikos, RN, EOLS, *The Quietus House LLC*

"I wish I'd had this journal when I became a school leader 30 years ago! The leadership mantle can be difficult for women to comfortably wear while maintaining their own sense of self and strength. These reflective questions can help center a new leader or one trying to keep her momentum mid-career or someone like myself redefining goals in retirement. This journal and your answers can help solidify your style and strengths as you move forward in your personal or professional goals."

—Jean Jordan

"Phyllis writes a great tool for actualizing one's dreams and loving the process. I am recommending this book to my clients."

—Jeffrey Levine, Chief Strategist, *Dr. Get in Focus*

"Phyllis' book emulates all that she is—her purpose! I couldn't put the manuscript down. Get ready for a spiritual experience that is destined to help you become the person you want to be. 'So, stop keeping your dreams to yourself. Shout them with conviction, and let your deeds mirror your thoughts. Trust and believe me, others who admire you are watching. They are also waiting for you to invite them into your dream. Without others, our dreams are just unanswered aspirations. You need others to move your dream to reality.' Simply put—OUTSTANDING!"

—Stacie Stanley, Superintendent, *Edina Public Schools*

"This book had me at week one! 'Do you want to be right or be effective?' Having had the opportunity to be in the space of learning and reflection with Phyllis, I will never forget the day she said these words to me. Seems simple right? This book is a gift of insight that everyone needs to reflect on how their actions are impacting their lives, relationships, and effectiveness in achieving their goals."

—Janet Gracia, Chief Culture Officer, *Girl Scouts of Minnesota and Wisconsin River Valleys*

"Be Right or Be Effective, is a great journal guide to help me get to new levels in many areas of my life. Phyllis Braxton gives of herself in a highly vulnerable space, which teaches humility is a huge step towards fulfilling dreams. The 'Wisdom Guides' along with the '5 A's' for each week are great motivation to get up, get started, and get moving in my purpose. Thank you, Phyllis."

—Kerri Lewis, Associate Pastor, *Faith Tabernacle Gospel Fellowship International*

"Beautiful, wise, inviting. This book is a fantastic look at the complex relationship we each have with success and imposter syndrome. Phyllis shares wisdom guides she has developed on these subjects and offers a wonderful peek at some tools we can use to step into our full self."

—Jon-Luke West, Director of Engineering, *HomeSeer*

"My favorite takeaways are:
1.) Embrace your unique quirks
2.) Open up to others' gifts
3.) You are not a movement (see #2)
4.) Legacies are important
5.) The Platinum Rule is the bomb
6.) Relationships are what it's all about (being right isn't as rewarding as being effective)
Give yourself the gift of digging into this insightful guide to creating the life you want."

—Martie McNabb, Founder & Chief Story-sharing Host, *Thingtide Show & Tales LLC*

"There is a reason so many people gravitate toward Phyllis Braxton—her charisma and no-nonsense approach to all things is a breath of fresh air! *Be Right or Be Effective* is a wonderful tool for anyone looking to reflect deeply on how to take control of their lives and establish ultimate happiness."

—Roseanne Cheng, Co-founder, *Evergreen Authors*

"Phyllis' writing comes across as joyful, confident, generous, humble, authentic, vulnerable, inspiring, and brilliant! Dig in."

—Omkar Sawardekar, Therapist, Trainer, Intercultural Coach, & Consultant

"Phyllis Braxton offers thoughtful, compassionate, and authentic wisdom in her new book, *Be Right or Be Effective: A 30-Day Journey to Mastering Life's Messes and Unexpected Challenges*, and it's just what many of us need right now. The '5 A's' in the journal section allows readers to give deep thought and inspired action in creating success. We all go through challenges, and the lessons that Phyllis outlined helped her to create this meaningful and effective wisdom."

—Caryn Warren, CEO, *SHE CAN DO I.T.*

"Guide that engages readers in 30 days to be more mindful of the actions they take to get where they want to go on their own life's adventure."

—Donna Adinolfi, CEO, *Mindful Adventures*

A 30-Day Journey to Master Life's Messes and
Overcome Unexpected Challenges

BE RIGHT

OR BE

EFFECTIVE

a journal by
Phyllis D. Braxton

BE RIGHT OR BE EFFECTIVE

A 30-DAY JOURNEY TO MASTER LIFE'S MESSES AND OVERCOME UNEXPECTED CHALLENGES

A journal by
Phyllis D. Braxton,
LGSW, MSW, MEd

Be Right or Be Effective: A 30-Day Journey To Master Life's
Messes And Overcome Unexpected Challenges

For booking the author, Phyllis D. Braxton:
Contact: Pink Consulting, LLC | PinkConsultingLLC.com

For publisher information contact:
Claxco Publishers
950 Eagles Landing Pkwy #263 | Stockbridge, GA 30281
GoClaxco.com

Book Layout and Cover Design by Claxco Media, LLC.
ISBN-Paperback: 978-0-9827738-6-4
First Edition: December 2022
10 9 8 7 6 5 4 3 2 1

FIRST EDITION

DEDICATION

To God, my creator, I give you all the glory, honor, and praise.

To my parents, Viola and Sammie Braxton, you gave me the best foundation for life beyond your means. I will do all within my power to ensure you both have a life that's well and fully lived.

To my siblings, you are the wind beneath my wings. Without your support, I know my life would be different.

To my mentors, for your investment in me; I am beyond grateful.

To my colleagues, you make me better and hold me accountable.

To my closet friends, you keep me anchored, motivated, and true to myself.

To my best friend, Allison Barnett Howze, thank you for seeing "it" in me for the past 30 years before I owned "it" for myself.

To my daughter, Ivy Zaire, you are my biggest cheerleader and conscious compass.

To my husband Marcus, you are my rock, my heart healer, and my future.

And, to me! For finally realizing at 50 that I do not have to pretend to be who I already am –

absolutely brilliant!

SPECIAL ACKNOWLEDGEMENTS

To the sophisticated women of Alpha Kappa Alpha Sorority, Inc., for an undying sisterhood of support.

To Oprah, for illuminating that a po' lil' Black girl from small town Mississippi can dream more than one dream.

To Toby Egan, Beth Zemsky, Nehrwr Addul-Wahid, Julius Erolin, Brian Wise, Bob Johnson, Dr. Mitch Hammer, Dr. Milton Bennet, and the late Jim Fields for indoctrinating my intellectual and pedagogical DEI foundation.

To Morris Brown College, for my foundation of coming into the complexity of "my" Blackness and my academic self-reliance and assurance.

To the University of Minnesota for turning on my love of practical theories and research.

To the Urban League organization, for giving me my first career track full-time exempt opportunity that led to my DEI interests.

To the Girl Scouts for encouraging my confidence by investing in me as a girl and women.

To my spiritual leaders and community, thank you for always "RE-filling" my cup.

To St. Catherine University/University of St. Thomas for challenging me to my highest academic capacity and accountability while balancing support to my differing social, emotional, and biological needs while accomplishing one of my dreams.

To Fielding Graduate University and my doctoral professors for refusing to let me fail myself.

To my clients, for entrusting me with your greatest assets — your human resources.

To my PINK Partners, PINK does not thrive without you.

To Natasha Cozart, for being the divine right partner to propel the PINK Brand into the future.

To my mental wellness team, you taught me to learn through tough times and grow through self-doubt to break through to authentic joy.

To my PINK Team, Essence and Allison, only you know!

TABLE OF CONTENTS

INTRODUCTION

"It's about damn time!" My mouth dropped in shock as I heard these words shriek from the lips of a person I had admired and who ushered me into my career. A new surge of conflicting emotions flooded my heart as the relationship admiration and respect between us being there was something deeper. The feeling was more like reverence for him in the field of diversity, equity, and inclusion (DEI). Which is why I care about what he thought or if he even thought I would be ready.

Hearing him say it was "about damn time" – touched my spirit in a way that propelled me to step out on not just faith but also the foundation that I had built for myself in the industry over the past ten years of my career.

Right there in the first booth by the kitchen at Joe's Crab Shack, PINK was born. What's pink got to do with it?

See, "what had happened was" my position was being eliminated from the company where I worked for seven years. It was really no surprise, as many companies sign on to diversity, equity, and inclusion work for a couple of years, check the boxes and then resort back to business as usual.

However, I was fortunate enough to be a part of the conversation about my role being eliminated. My leader at the time, Jim Fields and Brother Milton Barker (bless their souls), encouraged me to step out on my own and gave me the agency to do so.

So, after seven years of doing DEI work for a statewide organization, I made the scariest phone call ever to my mentor and friend, Nehrwr Abdul-Wahid. I asked if he could meet me as I wanted to talk with him about the next steps for my career.

When he greeted me, and I told him I was thinking of starting my own company, his green eyes lit up like a light bulb. I'll never forget it. He said, "About damn time."

What came next, I still laugh about to this day. He said, "whatever you name your company, it's gotta have something to do with pink. You wear it all the time."

Then he said, "It (PINK) could stand for Pursuing Intercultural," then I added, "Needs & Knowledge." BOOM! Right there in that booth at Joe's Crab Shack, the concept of PINK Consulting, LLC was born.

For those wondering what the heck DEI work is, DEI stands for diversity, equity, and inclusion. I provide intercultural competency training, intercultural assessments, trauma-informed coaching, and keynote and motivational speaking worldwide across any industry. Basically, I develop the human unconsciousness in a developmental way so people's good intentions and impact on others align.

For me, pink is not just a color; it is an outlook on life. Pink is kind of its own thang and complex, like me. Some would even say it's not an actual color or that it is a hue of red. Well, It's just not a spectral color, which means it isn't found in the spectrum of pure colors that form when you split white light with a prism. In other words, pink can be an illusion, much like life. The color combination of pink (and green) is my favorite because of the meaning it has for my connection to my sorority, Alpha Kappa Alpha, Incorporated. Oh yeah, and I look damn good in all shades of it. LOL!

Another thing about the color Pink, it's also my company uniform. Owning my own business means I'm always working, so I wear a lot of pink clothing. I am a connoisseur of all shades of pink. I've been wearing it on purpose for over 30 years now. I see pink more complexly than most. It always amazes me when a person plays the "I got you" game with me regarding a shade of pink I'm wearing. I've heard such things as, "Wow, Phyllis, you're wearing purple today instead of pink." When this occurs, I think, "Hmm, how do I want to respond?"

I respond with a smile and soft voice, "thank you for noticing my wardrobe. I appreciate that note- fun fact: this color's name is chocolate raspberry – it's in the pink family. Interesting how it can look purple also, huh?" After I am out of sight, I shake my head. I really want to say, "do you think I would name my company PINK and brand it as such, and I show up in purple?"

Just like the pink hue is complex, so is life. Now that you know a little about what I do, I want to share with you more about the person I've become as a result of what I do.

Turning 50 is different for everyone. For me, it's been liberating and overwhelming at the same time. It was liberating because I am no longer willing to minimize or mold myself to please other people. Also, somewhat overwhelming because I've been doing that for nearly 50 years. Frankly speaking, which is my intention between these pages, it's scary being on the other side of 50 years of life. Yes, more humans live past 100 with a relatively good quality of life, but when you turn 50, 100 seems way closer than at 49.

Although life "ain't been no crystal stair", I am blessed. I am beyond blessed because, at 50, I've realized more of my dreams for my life than this lil' Black girl from Moss Point, Mississippi, could have ever thought possible. My success and my failures have led me to think about my thinking. It's called phenomenology. Yup, I'm geeky like that. I love thinking about how the human experience unfolds and the theory of human change.

How do we go through situations and learn from them at that moment but not retain the practice lifelong? You should know any question I pose to you in this journal, I first asked myself. Writing this journal has held me to some values and principles that I was wise enough to use in a moment but missing the opportunity to share lifelong lessons with others. That got me

4

thinking about the difference between being wise and having wisdom.

Being wise can be described as the mode of action taken when making decisions during circumstantial events using the knowledge learned from a previous experience or used in a current moment of interaction to become more effective or get the results you want.

Being wise is a consistent circumstantial behavior, a moment-to-moment occurrence. Being wise is first a cognitive act – you obtain the knowledge. Next, your behavior should consistently be in keeping with the value.

Being wise is an embodiment of practice that becomes your norm, habit, or primary way of engaging in the world. Being wise is not a one-off occurrence; it is the anchoring of how you consistently navigate your most difficult interactions and decisions. Being wise is knowledge manifested in unwavering behavior.

In contrast, wisdom is shared but not always practiced. The life experiences I will share with you can therefore be summed up in a word whose description reaches beyond the category of "life lessons," they are my instructional principles that keep me centered and consistent within the ever-changing landscape of life. I call them "Wisdom Guides." Although I can share wisdom and knowledge with you until I'm blue in the face, you must practice these guides to develop more effective interactions with others. Then and only then are you wise.

To open my world and share these guides with you, through my post-it notes, failed journal attempts, iPhone notes, voice recordings, and thoughts written on random pieces of paper could only get me so far. I had to write all this Sugar Honey Iced Tea down.

I'm 50 and forgetting a lot - a lot more often. Let me be clear beyond measure. I am not a saint. I'm still working my issues out, also. I also share this because, hopefully, that's another reason you picked up this journal. Because you, like me, are human and a work in progress. There is no way I would hold myself to an unreasonable expectation of practicing all of these "Wisdom Guides" simultaneously. At most, human brains can only practice 3-5 in any given situation.

This book is the coming together of my reflections on love, loss, success, and failure. At 50, I've learned a lot, and I rise daily to greet the new lessons that await. I've learned to laugh just a little faster and to practice radical acceptance of self from 50 years of life filled with trials and triumphs.

My most vulnerable losses have led to these reflections that I attribute to saving my family, career, sanity, and spirit. Rebounding from my lowest points ultimately taught me to live a full life, moment by moment, and accept more quickly that the losses and disappointments are our divine life lessons.

This book will invite you to think deeply about your own life's transitions. Additionally, the journal is designed to process the impact those transitions have on how you treat others and give you a roadmap to activate the light inside of you to live into your deepest values with empathy and a renewed sense of purpose.

I humbly offer that we do not learn about ourselves by ourselves. It is the interactions with others that can make us (or should make us) hold up a mirror to see our own streaks before we look through the window to see the streaks of others. Start with self.

First, we must turn inward and get wildly curious about ourselves, why we do the things we do, and how we do them, then turn outward and seek other perspectives to add to our awareness and inform our actions. These reflections, coupled with action, have been life-changing for me.

I have discovered that when I choose a mindset of effectiveness versus being right, I build more relational glue that deepens the connection to move forward where all involved feel seen, heard, and valued. I am wise enough to know that while I am special, I am not unique. I would be aloof if I thought I was the only person on earth who has faced adversity. In my experience through thousands of touchpoints with humans around the world, what makes me special is I have lived by a mantra that states, "Life is ten percent of what happens to you and ninety percent of how you respond." Through adverse childhood experiences, trauma, seen and unseen, disabilities, mental health challenges, imposter's syndrome, and just some outright terrible shit, I continue to choose life - an abundant life.

I hope something shared here will encourage you to heal yourself and your relationships. I want you to overcome imposter syndrome and self-doubt and transform into someone who embodies empathic leadership, masters maintaining meaningful relationships, and obtains success to live the life you desire for yourself. You deserve that life NOW!

If I'm Being Honest

I had a come-to-God conversation with myself and still needed an intervention. This book is the journal that almost wasn't. I have another book, Good Intentions, Bad Results: A Practical Guide to Building Intercultural Confidence and Healthier Relationships at Work, Home, and School (GIBR), that was supposed to be this book. See, what had happened was this pesky thing called imposter's syndrome that I have affectionately named "nuisance narratives" was on me strong.

There it was, sitting in my email, my assistant informed me. I immediately logged in and scrolled down to the email, and what happened next shocked the shit out of me. I froze. I absolutely could not move my wrist to guide my hands to move my fingers to double-click. I was freaking afraid. Of what, you ask? The fully edited version of my manuscript for GIBR.

You see, this journal was written in six days because I waited over a month before I opened the damn email from my editor for GIBR, so of course, that threw off the release date. What is equally true is that I had a world-renowned location already agreed for my December engagement, which could also serve as the launch for my book. If you haven't put it together yet, I have an opportunity out of this world – but no damn book! This challenge was the catalyst for what I will share next. The two "Wise Guides" that my mentor, colleague, friend, and author of PIOOYA Principles, Nehrwr Abdul-Wahid, taught me. These principles keep me sane and productive.

PIOOYA Principle #1: Problem, not a Catastrophe!

Listen, in my work, I am consistently faced with problems, but the world is not ending as a result. Therefore, they are simply problems and not a disaster. Guess what y'all? Didn't I just say I solve problems every day? You do too. So, what are your possible solutions if this isn't the end of the world? I believe there is almost always more than one correct answer. This journal was my solution. It was one right answer to fulfill one of my dreams. Now, here's the thing. I was lucky. The definition I have adopted for "lucky" is when preparedness meets opportunity—I got that from my girl, Oprah. Wink, wink. Holla back, O if you hear me. Pardon my manners, "Queen O., Okay?" I'm a fan, follower, and friend. She just doesn't know it yet.

Let's talk about this luck thang for a minute. Because I had a dream of writing a book like I had been preparing for the last ten-plus years. I was capturing my thoughts and learnings from church sermons to scenes from the Young & the Restless, from Intellectuals like Dr. Micheal Eric Dyson to the comedic stylings of Chris Rock. Pause for a second I'm about to get geeky with you. I'm pausing because I noticed my last two examples were both men. Hmmm, why is that? I am a feminist! Why didn't

8

women come to mind first? Yeah, yeah, yeah, they're also both Black. That was intentional in my thinking. You see, this is what I mean about I love thinking about our thinking. I promise you; you don't want to live in my head.

Sorry for the detour; let's get back to the wisdom principle. I dreamed of publishing this journal when I was ready to share more of myself with people who know me and a new audience. Given that I am a somewhat private person, most people who think they know me really don't. So of course, I ran from the thought of the vulnerabilities I share on these pages as being my first book out there for the world to see "my stuff." That's when GIBR was born, so my first book would be more DEI-related, a relatively safer public entry as an author and building the PINK brand. And what do you know, the book that wasn't supposed to be first is. The universe humors me in that way.

Fun fact, even this journal almost wasn't. Again, to reiterate, see what had happened was, I had my heart set on this book being named 50 Lessons You Must Master Before 50. Cool right? I'll keep that idea on the shelf. I had over 50 "Wise Guides," but I could not produce 50 stories in six days while working and being a full-time student, mother, and wife. You can see how that would be a problem, right? You may think I may have been tempted to give up! Well, hell-to-the-naw, you must shift with the shit life serves you. I was sharing my problem with a daily check-in buddy, and she gave me a revelation. It's my book, and I can have it my way. No one else knows it was supposed to be 50. Again, I could have gone straight for catastrophe, but I sought help [remember, you cannot do it ALL alone], and the problem was solved.

Wherever you are in life right now, breathe. Give yourself consent to invest in yourself over the next 30 days. You are worth it.

PIOOYA Principle #2: Accept Limitations

Most of my close friends and family would say I'm good at many things; organizing is not one of them. Everyone cannot be good at everything. As a person with dyslexia, I've had to practice radical acceptance that I am not a good organizer, reader, or speller, not even decent or close. I've always known my brain worked differently since I was little. You can only imagine how those limitations might impact my ego as a highly educated woman. I've accepted those flaws, but they don't mean failure in life. I know now that I must operate differently, which requires me to work much harder in some areas of life. Thank God for spell check, autocorrection, and speak-to-text.

In context, my spelling is so bad that when I surprised myself and spelled catastrophe correctly, I thought something was wrong with my computer because the red line never appeared. What's worse is that after a red line did not appear under the word, I was so uncertain that I stopped writing to look up "catastrophe" in the dictionary. I surprised myself. You must understand how huge that was for me. Yes, I was on cloud nine for a couple of days. What I learned is that I need to trust myself more academically.

Given that I lived for over 40 years with undiagnosed dyslexia, I certainly have the nuisance narrative on the brain. Moreover, I don't have much evidence to substantiate my fear. I graduated in the top 4% of my class in high school. I was academically ranked number 24 of 404. I graduated from undergrad with a 3.0 GPA (but I partied hard). I finished my first master's degree with a 3.8 GPA, my second master's with a 3.4, passed the licensure exam on the first try, and I currently have a 3.5 in my doctoral program. I even got an A in statistics. And I struggled, clawed, and cried many a day. Can I get a "GO ON, girl?"

I used to feel less than and even dumb until I was 43 and got an official diagnosis. Once I knew my shortcomings, I could take action and give myself permission to seek support. Rarely does anyone get through life totally alone, so why was there an aroma of shame in the air for me? Well, I am going to tell you. Hear me and hear me now. Please don't wait until you're over 50 to embrace your weaknesses as unique quirks that the creator gifted specifically to you. It's up to you how you use those gifts to influence others and have a positive footprint in the world. Remember, there are others with your inadequacies, and they are waiting on you to show up and show out.

I know with great certainty that I can accomplish almost anything I set my intentions on with hyper focus and consistent actions. Usually, those are things that I am highly interested in, and some knowledge about and my differing abilities don't hinder me from doing them with ease. Typically, I get some enjoyment from doing it, like learning how to make balloon arches from YouTube during Covid. I love creating them. However, I would never want to do it for income. It has become a requested gift from my friends and family. In short, I loved learning how to do it. I love that there is a beginning, middle, and end. I love the authentic appreciation shown to me every time I gift it.

Here I go getting geeky again. It amazes me how something that brings me joy and a sense of accomplishment totally stresses my husband out. When I bring out my electric balloon pump, I can see him huffing and puffing under his breath with disdain. It makes me laugh out loud just writing about it. Even after having a very transparent conversation about why I enjoy doing it, he still responds negatively. How can that be? I mean, it's only balloon arches, man. That fascinates me.

That being said, at 50, I'm not trying to work hard at things that do not bring me joy. What and who the hell for? Whatever your limitations, accept them, and if you absolutely have to do something you don't enjoy, get support. You'd be surprised how many people in your network would love the opportunity to help you. Remember, more often than not, that nuisance narrative is whispering to you. You are the only one who expects you not to be unsurpassable in every area of your life. Do more of what you love. Start by reflecting and renewing your thinking first. This journal will help.

What's In This Journal

Bestow yourself the next 30 days to give back to you. In doing so, everyone you encounter will benefit. Each week there is a theme. Every weekday there is a "Wisdom Guide," with commentary and prompts for you to complete. On the weekends, you will reflect on your mindset and your own "Wise Guides." Before you know it, you will reflect, reground, renovate, reset, repair, renew, restart, and get results in the relationships and accomplishments that are important to you. My brilliant and wicked-smart mentor led me to these wise words. "You are not a movement; what's inside of you that people can be a part of is [a movement]."

If I profess something is a great idea, that's just me blowing my own horn. If others who have bought into my mission say it's a great idea, now we are talking about impact. If you have goals to change the world, you are gonna need a fan club. In other words, you need a critical enough mass of other people singing your song. So much so that your songs become their song.

I am always amazed at how an artist can ignite a movement with the words of a song. Think about your favorite song. It's the one that comes on the radio, and you immediately turn it up and start singing along at the top of your vocal cords. What makes you do that? What has been your story that artist tapped into? What values, beliefs, or experiences did that artist communicate to you through their song? Your answer to all those things is what you need to make others care about what you care about deeply.

So, stop keeping your dreams to yourself. Shout them with conviction, and let your deeds mirror your thoughts. Trust and believe me, others who admire you are watching. They are also waiting on you to invite them into your dream. Without others, our dreams are just unanswered aspirations. You need others to move your dream to reality.

Setting Your Intentions

Can you recall a dream or goal you have for yourself that you've never shared or said out loud? How has that worked out for your success in accomplishing it?

_____

_____

_____

_____

_____

_____

Looking forward, name one dream you have that you cannot accomplish alone or even with several people. How could shifting to a movement mindset change the outcome of your life, family, or career?

_____

_____

_____

_____

_____

What barriers can you anticipate getting in the way of completing this journey? What solutions can you anticipate?

13

_____

_____

_____

_____

_____

_____

In 30 days, I will:

_____

_____

_____

You don't have to come to your wisdoms alone. Allow me to share and guide you to your own wisdoms that will change your life. Also, you will be tempted to read the entire book in a day. If you must — do so. And I suggest that you give yourself at least a day for each Wisdom Guide. In fact, take an entire week if you want. You will get the most out of this journey when you allow yourself to reflect, sit with and hold your experiences for the richness they bring. It is only when we truthfully and fully face our obstacles that change can and will happen.

This journal consists of a framework I created as a pathway to your wise moments for life.

- Wisdom Guide

- Acceptance: the realities we cannot change

- Acknowledge: how that reality shows up

- Application: of cognitive awareness

- Activation: in behavior

- Affirmation: to stay consistent

14

WEEK ONE:
RE-FLECT & RE-GROUND

I believe each of us was put here for a purpose. Have you discovered yours yet? What justification do you have for your time here on earth? Why are you here? What legacy are you leaving for the known and unknown? If you have not discovered or confirmed your purpose with your creator, this is the time! Without purpose, we cannot live on purpose. What does it mean to live on purpose? It means you take steps, no matter how small, on a consistent basis to fulfill your destiny in this realm in this lifetime.

This week, you will get in touch with yourself and your purpose. This process is a must, especially if you are over 50. Legacies are not created overnight. The sooner you are grounded in your purpose, the sooner you can start leaving footprints for your impact in the world. Reflection is the key to learning, unlearning, and relearning messages taught to us explicitly and implicitly since birth. Those messages have turned into an internalized monologue with yourself. Those messages can be both positive and negative. Trust me when I say one side will win. And, you get to play a role in whether your purpose propels you and others to be better or interferes with and blocks yours and their success.

Give yourself this time to reground, even if you've never felt grounded before today. Time waits for no one. Now is your time to get clear on what you desire for your future, your life, your family, and your career. If you want to know how I've gained the success I currently have, which ain't too shabby, be a full participant in your growth and development. Within these pages, I share the wisdom of my wise moments. It's up to you to be open to change. It's up to you if these wisdom guides move from being merely inspirational to operational. Do not let this journal join all the other good-intentioned attempts at genuinely changing your life and possibly the world.

Let's get started!

DAY 1: WISDOM GUIDE #1

TO CHANGE THE WORLD – START WITH YOU

Acceptance:

As a diversity, equity, and inclusion master practitioner and coach, I get to know a lot of people from all kinds of backgrounds at a very intimate level, very quickly and in a short amount of time. One pattern of human behavior I have observed with intention over the last 25 years is that rarely are people willing first to look within and think how they may have contributed to the challenges, lack of success, or just outright dysfunction before contributing it to another party.

I was working with a cross-functional team whose end goal was student success. I was invited to work with the team to create a healthy, reciprocal, and high-functioning team across three departments with three not-so-distinct roles. I met with each department separately to discover and categorize their unique issues, and to also gain a better understanding of the best method to tame the issues they were having. The most unambiguous theme was that each group loved working with each other but had challenges working with members of the different departments. Each department pointed at each other and their leaders as to who and what the root causes were. There was blame being thrown around like a hot potato. I cannot count how many buses the leader got thrown under repeatedly. It was a hot mess up in there.

Honestly, I felt stuck on what the next best step was. After pondering it for about a week, I devised a plan. I first had to communicate with the group, confirm what I heard them say, and obtain agreement or clarity if I missed something. The next step was the kicker. I had to get the group to discover that they were

18

taking no part of the responsibility for their lack of trust, dysfunction, and outright dislike for each other.

You see, when you tell adults something, you own it; when you give them an opportunity to discover it for themselves, they can own it. To heal and move forward, this group would have to take personal responsibility for how their behavior exacerbates their challenges.

The point here is this group wanted organizational change without changing themselves. Please do not think this client has a monopoly on projecting onto others without and before doing a self-check. On the most basic level, most change starts with you, not the other person. This principle is definitely a wisdom that requires you to ask yourself, do I want to be right, or do I want to be effective? Do I want to be heard, or do I want to be understood and get results? Do I want to inflame the conflict further, or do I want community, connection and change?

If you want to be effective, more self-awareness is key. Being attuned to how your lack of success intersects with your culture, personality, and biological makeup is pivotal. Is your tendency to first look more critically at the other party rather than yourself when challenges arise? To date, one of my most powerful therapy sessions was when my therapist asked me this question.

"What role did your thinking or behavior contribute to the issue, and how is it serving you?"

That question shifted my core so much that I was initially overly crucial of myself in every conflictual situation. I would own it all. Even when I felt strongly that the other party was at fault, I would hold and own their part. Over the years, I have developed more balance regarding what I own in any given situation. By understanding my own patterns of behavior, I am better able to change myself first. Then and only then should I communicate my needs and expectations to the other party.

Acknowledge: What is one specific change you desire in your life, your career, or in the world? When you look for the change you want in others first, versus yourself, how has that worked out for you?

_____

_____

_____

_____

_____

_____

Application: Focus on one change you want in your life. What is one thing you can change about yourself first before expecting change in others?

_____

_____

_____

_____

_____

_____

Activation: What words, symbols, analogies, icons, memes will you use to shift your thinking and behavior in the future?

_____

_____

_____

_____

_____

_____

Affirmation: I truly am the change I want to see in the world so I will set the expectation and be a model for that change. I will see that change in my lifetime.

DAY 2: WISDOM GUIDE #2

YOU MUST SEE YOURSELF THERE
BEFORE YOU GET THERE

Acceptance:

In "Wisdom Guide #17", "no such thing is a small thing," I share several things about my life's quests. I knew when I was in my senior year of college while taking some English Language & Literature courses at Morehouse College (although I attended and graduated from Morris Brown College [shout out]) that I wanted to start a nonprofit that would bring equity to women and girls racially, educationally, and economically.

The idea was inspired by one of my Morehouse professors. I remember that feeling of truly being seen prophetically. I was often quiet in class (my friends can't imagine this), but I was writing my ass off. I was consistent at getting my assignments in always at a high level. This professor saw me, more like he poured into me.

See what had happened was he saw my yearbook and asked if he could sign it. I'm so glad he did because I didn't have the courage to ask him. What he wrote was a part of the change in my life trajectory, hopes, and dreams. Seems dramatic? Just thinking about it gives me chills, and I'm reminded of the impact of our individual power, especially educators.

He shared in my yearbook that he saw me becoming the founder and head of my own educational institution. I was like, "Say, huh, say what?" Lil ole me-raised in a small town in Mississippi by cotton sharecroppers? Do you mean the girl with undiagnosed dyslexia? Do you mean the girl that has to "re-re-re-read" most things? The girl that has only read three books in their entirety to date (shhh, don't judge me, I'm dropping some vulnerability on y'all)? Yes, me! Why not me?

He planted a seed when I was 21 years old. At 50 and two-third years, I realized that dream on October 13, 2022, when wholeSOUL, Inc (https://wholesoulinc.org/) was born. As founder and executive director, wholeSOUL, Inc will serve marginalized women and girls because of race, class, and education. wholeSOUL, Inc envisions a world where women and girls thrive through mental wellness, education, and philanthropy. Our mission is to educate, coach, and facilitate mindsets and skill sets for women and girls to prosper.

All of that to say, a seed was planted, and I began, at that moment, visualizing myself as the founder and head of an institution. Well, look at God; won't He do it? From that one seed, I have accomplished several dreams. None are a coincidence. I saw myself here before I got here. Where is here? For me, "here" was rigorous academic pursuit. Becoming the founder and head of an educational institution meant I would need more education under my belt. I was intentional. I sought out the next opportunity to pursue my master's degree. It happened to find me at Morris Brown. I attended an informational session, applied, and received a full scholarship to attend the University of Minnesota. That education led me to work long enough to acquire the experience needed to be a people leader.

From those experiences, 17 years ago, I sent out an email to 100 people informing them of my stepping out to start my consulting practice. That was the last time I solicited business. Now after training, coaching, and educating leaders of leaders across industries across the world, I acquired the skills I needed to start my nonprofit. This accomplishment was not luck. I labored for it.

Think about what it takes to be intentional for 30 years. All because someone saw something within me that I could not see in myself at the time. All the accomplishments I mentioned were not a shock or surprise to me; they were like homecomings. I had already seen myself there before I got there. Very few people are lucky and stumble upon success without intentionality. The rest of us have to be strategic and premeditated.

Don't believe me, try it. Start with something small like waiting for a parking space. Instead of speaking what you don't want – speak into the universe what you do want. Visualize yourself parked close to the entrance. Practice with me, "there is a park for me; thank you for my parking space near the entry," and repeat. This practice is a concept I learned when I read (some of) The Secret. "Dang, Phyllis. That is a short book." See, look at me judging myself. Thank goodness I'm a work in progress, and there is no way in hell I can practice all of these "Wisdom Guides" at the same time. I practice this concept with everyday things that life throws at me. It keeps nuisance narratives out of my head.

Acknowledge: Recall a time when you visualized yourself being successful? How did that work out for you? Did you take any actions towards that success?

_____

_____

_____

_____

_____

Application: Take a minute right now and give yourself permission to dream for yourself, your family and your life. And take the necessary steps to achieve that vision, how would life, family and your career be different?

_____

_____

_____

_____

_____

Activation: What words, symbols, analogies, icons, memes will you use to shift your thinking and behavior in the future?

_____

_____

_____

_____

_____

Affirmation: Success is mine. Whatever I put my mind and deeds to will return exponential benefits.

DAY 3: WISDOM GUIDE #3

WHEN YOU ARE WALKING IN YOUR PURPOSE, ALL COMPETITION CEASES TO EXIST

Acceptance:
When I am my highest self in challenging situations, I pause and ask myself, "Phyllis, who are you in competition with?"

What is a challenging situation? An interaction that still occupies mental, emotional, spiritual, and psychological space.

Who/what is the competition? Anyone or any entity to which you compare your success.

When you approach your success with intentions of the best possible outcomes, you do not compare yourself against others; you compare yourself to your best you. A'int that some Suga Honey Iced Tea for ya? My Mississippi roots are showing up now.

I distinctly remember coming to this revelation during a sermon by my Sr. Pastor, Dr. E. Mae Beecham, one Sunday. My brain and body were trying to take in what was being professed. If I'm being honest, one of my first thoughts was – oh my goodness, this means I must stop comparing myself to others. If there is no comparison, there is no competition.

My purpose is for me and me alone. In 25 years, I've witnessed many people do what I do, and I am assured in saying that no one can or will deliver it into the universe like me. Sounds conceited? Possibly. But I offer up being convinced. When you know your purpose, you are clearer about activating your life's mission and getting out of other people's lane.

Acknowledge: Do you tend to compare yourself and where you are in life right now to others? How is that working for you?

_____

_____

_____

_____

_____

_____

Application: If you focused on your life's mission as if you are the only one who can do it, how would things be different?

_____

_____

_____

_____

_____

_____

Activation: What words, symbols, analogies, icons, memes will you use to shift your thinking and behavior in the future?

_____

_____

_____

_____

_____

_____

Affirmation: I am my own competition. I am the only one who can deliver my purpose like I was created to do. I commit to staying focused on my lane. My success will be accelerated as a result.

DAY 4: WISDOM GUIDE #4

YOUR PURPOSE IS PERPETUAL

Acceptance:
At 50, this is what I know: There is nothing new under the sun. We are all special but not unique. In translation, other people can and will do what you do. It's like the universe has a backup plan. "The U-NI-VERSE will never be defeated!" Let me make it plain. If I am walking in my purpose, doors, windows, and sometimes cracks are opened to advance my dreams. It is the same for you. Your greatness will continue to evolve. And, after you've passed on, I hope you will have touched another soul to carry on. That's how your purpose will leave a deathless legacy and that's as perpetual as it gets.

Again, I work in the DEI field, and I believe it's a calling. My work is spiritual to me. I cannot do it alone. Given I believe there is more than one way to the divine, I call on all the Gods in the work I do – it's intercultural – so it makes sense, right? I hope so, or I will probably do a lot of explaining myself to religious folks. I believe I am one of the best at what I do. Because I trust and believe in myself, and because I value the positive feedback I have received, I know I have not experienced the height of my success. Because the universe sees I'm on the right track, she does not have to send out other entities with my purpose at this moment in time. And so, it goes. My purpose in life will be fulfilled, if not by me, by someone else.

So, here's the thing. If you survived Covid, "Get busy living or get busy dying" in my Morgan Freeman Shawshank Redemption voice. Yes, you are special and all, but if you don't get in your lane and make some traction, the universe will tap or create another you to get the job done. So, get your uniqueness in cue so you can become someone special in your desired sphere of influence.

Acknowledge: Name other people or entities that do what you do? The ones that do it on a global scale, what is the difference that's making a difference?

_____

_____

_____

_____

_____

Application: Take at least one of those differences and think through how and what you can learn from it for yourself. How could shifting to a perpetual mindset change the outcome of your life, family, or career?

_____

_____

_____

_____

_____

Activation: What words, symbols, analogies, icons, and memes will you use to shift your thinking and behavior in the future?

_____

_____

_____

_____

_____

Affirmation: I can fulfill my purpose in my time here on earth and leave an everlasting legacy as a result.

DAY 5: WISDOM GUIDE #5

DON'T LOOK LIKE WHAT YOU'RE GOING THROUGH

Acceptance:

Momma and daddy used to say, "look like you left the house on purpose." This one might get a little touchy because many know me to be a fashionista. In this wisdom, I am not talking about that kind of fashion, but fashion in the sense of, what's your trend? What's your pattern when you are going through something? How do you wear it in your energy, mindset, hygiene, and appearance?

One thing my clients cannot say about me is, "we were in person or at a virtual meeting with Phyllis, and she looked like a hot mess. I wonder what's going on with her?" The reality is that when my fibromyalgia got really bad, I had to share I wasn't feeling well. Because at any moment, I could experience pain so bad that I would damn near pass out. Their response was almost always, "Well, Phyllis, we sure wouldn't know it just by looking at you." Now, for some, this might seem disingenuous or even untruthful." As a Black, female entrepreneur, I don't have the privilege of showing up looking less than fabulous, at least to get the gig. The energy, tone, hygiene, and appearance I display are to show my clients respect.

If I cannot show up with the energy, I know that changes the environment for the good, I negotiate an alternative way to engage and communicate. Can we move that meeting from in-person to Zoom? Or, in Zoom, I'm going to need to be off-camera. Here's what usually happens. As an extrovert, I get energy from outside of me. So once I'm actually engaged in the meeting, my pain and health problems are non-detectible, because I am engaged in using my powers for good, rather than focusing on the nuisance narratives that would cause my fibromyalgia symptoms flare up anyways.

When going through difficulty, you have to do the very thing you dread. Facing it head-on to get control of it is often the cure. When I am in chronic pain, I have to make myself use those parts of my body. Before I was educated on my diagnosis, my entire body would be inflamed, and I couldn't get out of bed. After my diagnosis and education (thank God for The Mayo Clinic), I have not experienced 90% of the full-body flare-ups I did in the past. My fibromyalgia flares mostly attacked my wrists and hands, hips, ankles, and feet. To start, I would force myself to shower, knowing how much energy that would take even to try to hold the bath sponge. I learned to endure the dreadful temporary deep pain to only experience surface-level discomfort later. I marvel at how this works.

I don't know about you, but when I put effort into my outward appearance, I feel better inwardly. When you are down or experiencing challenges, I know it may be easier to disconnect from the world and give up. I advocate and urge you to do the opposite of how you feel at that moment. That challenge, that pain, that disappointment can't and won't last forever. And guess what? If you are feeling the pain, that means you are still alive, baby! And I guarantee, you won't see and experience a better day unless you make it through the night. Hang in there. Fight! You are worth it.

Acknowledge: Recall an area of your life that causes you anxiety or stress. Have you tried naming that thing before? How did that work out for you, and if you haven't how's that working out for you?

_____

_____

_____

_____

_____

_____

Application: If you are willing and able, try to think of other patterns of behavior that are associated with that stress. How could naming your thing change the outcome of your life, family, or career?

_____

_____

_____

_____

_____

_____

Activation: What words, symbols, analogies, icons, and memes will you use to shift your thinking and behavior in the future?

_____

_____

_____

_____

_____

_____

Affirmation: I will not be held back. I will hunt that thing down that's holding me back. I will name it. I will change it.

DAY 6: REFLECTION

Acknowledge: What highlights or insights did you gain?

_____

_____

_____

_____

_____

_____

Application: What is one concrete thing you can do differently?

_____

_____

_____

Activation: What do you need from yourself and others to make the change?

_____

_____

_____

_____

_____

Affirmation: What new thinking will you employ? Write your own encouragement to yourself. What is your affirmation?

_____

_____

_____

DAY 7: ACTION

What thinking and behaviors will you:

KEEP doing:

_____

_____

_____

_____

_____

_____

STOP doing:

_____

_____

_____

START doing:

_____

_____

_____

_____

_____

NOTES:

_____

_____

_____

WEEK TWO:
RE-NOVATE & RE-STORE

Now that you are grounded in your purpose or at least pondering, it is time to renovate and restore your confidence for the road ahead. Often, we get stuck in our nuisance narratives because of our past failures. This week you will work through turning mistakes into milestones toward your goals. Show me a person who has not made any mistakes, and I'll show you a unicorn or a narcissist.

Renovate means restoring to a good state of repair. Restore means to return to its original condition. It is time to decide what baggage you leave behind and what points from that pain you will decide to take with you into the future. As a recovering therapist, I know that many people in mental institutions could go home tomorrow if they forgive themselves for their past. This week you can decide if you want to use your mistakes as lessons or as the reasons that hold you back from living a full life.

Making mistakes is inevitable; it's how you recover that matters. This week take yourself on a journey to reflect on what messages you are holding onto from all your messes. I am not the first to say your past does not have to dictate your future. I know this to be true in my own life. As I mentioned earlier in this journal, I operate from a mindset that life is 10% of what happens to you and 90% of how you respond. This week take this time and be intentional about turning your missteps into growth milestones. Allow yourself to feel the pain, but don't miss the point.

DAY 8: WISDOM GUIDE #6

MAKING MISTAKES IS AN INDICATION THAT
YOU ARE STRIVING TOWARDS A GOAL

Acceptance:
Our current world has a culture of high expectations and perfectionism. So much so that it's paralyzing. Yes, even for me. I radically accept that I am a work in process, and I have to choose daily to take actions supporting progress.

There should be no shame in trying. We can miss our success from all the opportunities we don't take. Instead of focusing on what if I make a mistake, try to focus on how you can change the world and uplift humanity by taking the opportunity.

A mistake can make a mess or create something that has to be considered. Errors, faults, blunders, flaws, and oversights are just a few ways that a mistake can show up. Mistakes are vital if you are to become competent or proficient in anything. In fact, failure is a far better teacher than success. Succeeding at everything warrants no reflection; the focus becomes about the accolades, not the learning.

When a mistake is made, there is a reason for pausing and considering what could or should have been done differently. Now you are using a learner's mindset toward growth.

A willingness to try must be the mindset to develop the skillset.

Acknowledge: Does anticipating making mistakes paralyze your actions? How is that working for you? What if whatever you tried could NOT fail, how would your actions be different?

_____

_____

_____

_____

_____

_____

Application: Name a goal that you have been afraid to try or take that first step. What could be different in your life, your family or your career as a result?

_____

_____

_____

_____

_____

Activation: What words, symbols, analogies, icons, memes will you use to shift your thinking and behavior in the future?

_____

_____

_____

_____

_____

Affirmation: Mistakes are my steppingstones to make a difference in my life and in my career.

DAY 9: WISDOM GUIDE #7

MAKING MISTAKES ARE INEVITABLE;
LEARNING FROM THEM IS OPTIONAL

Acceptance:

I am a mistake-maker. If you are out there trying, so are you. The major difference is how you rebound. As a student of human behavior, I am amazed by the human response to making a mistake. For some, it's live and let live. These people make statements like, "Yeah, I made a mistake. Sue me."

For others, their actions say, "I am mortified I made a mistake. I am exiting stage left and hope the ground swallows me whole, so I don't have to deal with the consequences and shame. And, for some, but not the majority, we actually sit with the mistake, are curious about the negative outcome and the impact, and are determined to learn from it and change the behavior. Let me give you an example.

I decided to give myself a 50th birthday party weekend. Yes, two days of great music, dancing, live performances, and cake, of course! To create my invite list, I went to my excel spreadsheet from my big 40th birthday party.

Important note: until recently, I was not on social media. As an entrepreneur, small business owner, single mom, and full-time graduate student during those ten years, I was out of touch with my friends and colleagues.

I reached out by text message to a dear friend and colleague whom I had not connected with for some time. I wanted to get her mailing address to send a formal invitation to her and her life partner. Her reply stopped me in my tracks. Her partner had passed away. Yes, you can gasp with me.

That misstep could have paralyzed me forever. I had a choice to make at that moment. Make it about me, wallow in my mess, or learn and grow from it. Of course, I couldn't rebound instantly because shock and shame took over. Remember, I'm human. After I collected myself, I chose to practice what I preached. That conversation went something like this.

"Hi _____, I've had some time to reflect on our last text exchange, and I wanted to check in with you. I wanted to thank you and appreciate you for granting me the grace that I did not know _____ had passed. I need you to know that I value and care about our relationship. I want to reconnect more often because our friendship over the last 25-plus years has meant a lot to me. I am so sorry I've been so aloof. After you shared with me that _____ passed away, I was mortified that I had not been a good friend to you because that is a life event where I would have genuinely wanted to support you. I know people respond to the passing of a loved one differently. Do you mind me asking what your boundaries are for a conversation about _____?"

She responded with openness. I sincerely apologized for being out of touch and acknowledged how I could have handled the situation differently. We had a good time reconnecting. The energy was light. I checked in with her at the end of our conversation about our relational glue and our intentions moving forward. In fact, I'm overdue to reach out to her. Moving forward, I've learned as much as I dislike being on social media and the phone, they are shifts I need to make to use the information out there to support my approach with people I care about and love.

I offer up that the time is always right to do what's right. Instead of holding the guilt, shame, and disappointment in yourself, try being transparent with the person while focusing on your impact. Do not leave that conversation without knowing the state of your relationship with that person.

Acknowledge: Recall a time you made a mistake, and it paralyzed you? How did that work out for you? Were you able to rebound?

_____

_____

_____

_____

_____

_____

Application: What is one mistake you've made where there is still an opportunity to address it? How will you make your impact on the other person the focus and not your good intentions?

_____

_____

_____

_____

_____

_____

Activation: What words, symbols, analogies, icons, memes will you use to shift your thinking and behavior in the future?

_____

_____

_____

_____

_____

_____

Affirmation: My mistakes will manifest in an abundance of true and deeper relationships. Transparency, reciprocity, and inquiry is the way.

DAY 10: WISDOM GUIDE #8

STRUGGLES AND SUCCESS AREN'T FOR YOU ALONE; IT'S FOR THE PEOPLE THAT'S BEEN WATCHING AND WAITING ON YOU TO REALIZE IT FOR THEMSELVES

Acceptance:

Ever since I was a little girl, I have always felt this wind propelling me to stretch beyond what I knew and where I was. I always knew there was more to learn and more places to see than Moss Point, Mississippi. While I love the homey, small coastal town where I was born and raised, I also knew I needed a bigger container to play in to discover my purpose in the world.

If only I had a dollar for every time someone has commended me for being strong. Well, guess what? I don't want to be! I would never have signed up for all the S#*T I've been through in my life. I want to fall out in the streets and throw a temper tantrum like a 2-year-old, so someone can offer me a treat, give me a bath, lotion, powder me down with a fresh diaper, warm milk, and rock me to sleep.

For the majority of situations, I have faltered, I've felt like a fish in a bowl with the world watching. Sound dramatic? Well, that's just a glimpse at how anxiety works. While stressful and overwhelming at times, the feeling of being in the fishbowl with the world watching motivates me to REanchor, REthink, and REcover. Whether I like it or not, people look up to me, so they are watching and taking cues from me on how to push through it and share that wisdom when I come out on the other side.

Do not be fooled. You also have people with a strong interest in and admiration for you. They are paying attention to you. What would you tell or show them to leave them better than when you found them?

Acknowledge: Can you recall a time a person let you know how you handled a situation that inspired them? What did that feel like?

_____

_____

_____

_____

_____

_____

Application: Given the people you know are watching and waiting on you, what is the next best step you can model for them to push through their struggles and welcome their success?

_____

_____

_____

_____

_____

_____

Activation: What words, symbols, analogies, icons, and memes will you use to shift your thinking and behavior in the future?

_____

_____

_____

_____

_____

_____

Affirmation: The world is waiting on me. Here I come world.

DAY 11: WISDOM GUIDE #9

KEEP THE TROPHY. I WANT THE TITLE.

Acceptance:

Throughout this journal, you will learn that I love to dance. I am a part of a predominantly Black ballroom dance community that started in Chicago in the late 1940s to early 1950s. I would love to say that the culture is welcoming of you standing out if you have not earned it through the right teachers with the right tenure from the right part of town. To be fair, my Chicago 8 Count Stepping community is a great outlet for my mental health and physical well-being. But like most movements, there are disputes, rivals, back-stabbing, and back-biting. There's also backstage drama about who's partnering, who's in an entanglement, and of course, who's the best.

You should know, I am a competitive person. Not extremely competitive, but I don't like to lose. I'm usually a good sport when I do lose. However, when I really care, imagine the Rocky theme song playing on an awful loudspeaker. That's me coming! Loud and possibly irritating. I found that women in the Stepper's scene have a love-hate relationship with me. I sum it up to the fact that I'm being "the me" they want to be for themselves but hold back. Yup, I finally said it out loud. Over time, in one small club that I would frequent, me showing up looking like a million bucks and dancing with a sense of freedom and playfulness became a trend. Yup, I said it out loud. Me showing up how I did shifted that club's culture and clientele.

When I tell you I was addicted to this dance, I was a dancing, traveling, group learning, and private lessons taking "fiend" – my goal was mastery. I didn't want to do the dance for socializing; I aimed to be amongst the best at it. My actions were pursued accordingly. Within two years, I was on the big stage at the World's Largest Stepping Competition (WLSC) in Chicago – the mecca with the Heavy Hitters. I'm laughing to myself as I type these words because I have never written out the phrase Heavy Hitters. I am very imaginative, so I visualize a picture of a weight-heavy Black guy up to bat at a major league baseball game. I crack me up.

So let me school you on the lingo:
- *Steppin' or Stepping*: a predominantly Black Ballroom Dance Movement
- *Stepper:* one who steps (does a form of Steppin')
- *Stepper Set:* a coming together of steppers for the sole purpose of dancing
- *Heavy Hitter:* a dancer at the top of the charts, repetitive WLSC wins, well known across the country, usually an instructor, and has a following

My partner, J. Most and I took third place in the out-of-towners category. That means we beat out over 20 couples from all over the country except Chicago residents. So why was this a category? Well, because the dance was founded in Chicago. I don't know if you've heard the songs associated with the art form, but the lyrics speak for themselves. Steppin' is not just a dance; it's a way of life; it's a culture. Chicago and steppin' are like walking and chewing gum. It's a part of the DNA that runs through the Black communities there. It's the culture. That means steppers from Chicago usually have an advantage because of access and proximity to master instructors. They tend to produce a disproportionate amount of Heavy Hitters. That makes sense, right? Thus, I call Chicago the Mecca of Chicago 8 Count Steppin'.

That means if every category were open to everyone, more than likely, steppers from out-of-town probably would be at a disadvantage because of the lack of master instructors outside of Chicago. Therefore, there was an out-of-town category for everyone from somewhere other than Chicago. If you were competing at the WLSC, that means you've won a prelim in a certified, yes honey, certified Steppin' prelim competition held in different cities around the country.

All that to say, as a competitive person, the trophy nor the prize money [that we never received in full] meant nothing to me; I wanted a bigger title. Titles get you in doors and spaces that a participation trophy won't. Titles get you legacy, press, and awards that expand your potential to impact the world on a grander stage. Now go get your title.

Acknowledge: When was the last time you set your intentions on winning "the title" and you fell short of your goal? How did you rebound?

_____

_____

_____

_____

_____

Application: Think about a title, position, award, or acknowledgment that you desire. What is holding you back from pursuing it? How might your life, family, and career be different as a result?

_____

_____

_____

_____

_____

Activation: What words, symbols, analogies, icons, and memes will you use to shift your thinking and behavior in the future?

_____

_____

_____

_____

_____

Affirmation: There is no shame in seeking success. Success brings about a collective of believers for my cause. Those believers catapult my vision to others. With their help I make greater impacts in the world.

DAY 12: WISDOM GUIDE #10

WHATEVER IS HOLDING YOU BACK,
YOU MUST NAME IT TO TAME IT

Acceptance:

If some of my clients are activating this journal, they will nod up and down with a slow "oooooh, okaaaaaay." This thought is a more recent example of this learning. Here's the scoop. I rarely show up more than 15 minutes early for in-person gigs and 2 minutes for virtual ones. Why? I didn't really know why. I know timeliness is an important value to my clients and me. Still, I could not bring myself to get there any earlier unless they demanded it.

In a recent conversation with a colleague, I discovered "my why." My PINK Partner and I trained many people together with this particular client virtually. We learned one of the client's triggers was a rigid adherence to time. Therefore, when it was time to transition from virtual to in-person, it was no surprise that the request was to arrive one hour before the session. Now, I loved working with this client, and I was overjoyed by the thought of getting to see them in person after over three years. Long story short. We arrived an hour before, and the client was ecstatic.

My learning came in when the training was starting. By arriving that early and taking in all the things that could go wrong and did go wrong, but were fixed before the presentation began, jacked up my energy. Translation – not good. A person with diagnosed anxiety and already having to talk nuisance narrative off her shoulder does not need to know all the technical difficulties nor take on any negative energy from the participants. The bell started ringing so loudly in my ear.

I was subconsciously arriving close to my presentation time because I didn't realize how much anxiety I was bringing to my workshops with me. I tend to be pretty fearless, especially with large groups. This feeling was a revelation to me. Now that I named this thing, I can tame it.

How did you tame it, Phyllis? Here's another What Would Phyllis Do (WWPD) moment. I asked for what I needed. First, the next time I arrived an hour early, I immediately started to help set up the room. I needed something specific to focus on and direct my attention. Something easy, something I didn't have to think about, like putting handouts on tables. Next, I asked if there was anything specifically needed of me. There being none, I informed the training team that I would take a restroom break and get some fresh air. I dismissed myself and came back to the room about 10 minutes before to get any updates and make any adjustments.

LOL. Now some of the facilitators I work with would lose their shit if they could only get a tech update 10 minutes before a session. I am exceptionally flexible and adaptable when things go wrong, and you need to shift with it. I mention all of that to say for some people, not knowing would cause more anxiety. Two truths can exist at the same time, my friends.

Acknowledge: Recall an area of your life that causes you anxiety or stress. Have you tried naming that thing before? How did that work out for you, and if you haven't how's that working out for you?

_____

_____

_____

_____

_____

_____

Application: If you are willing and able, try to think of other patterns of behavior that are associated with that stress. How could naming your thing change the outcome of your life, family, or career?

_____

_____

_____

_____

_____

_____

Activation: What words, symbols, analogies, icons, and memes will you use to shift your thinking and behavior in the future?

_____

_____

_____

_____

_____

_____

Affirmation: I will not be held back. I will hunt that thing down that's holding me back. I will name it. I will change it.

DAY 13: REFLECTION

Acknowledge: What highlights or insights did you gain?

_____

_____

_____

_____

_____

_____

Application: What is one concrete thing you can do differently?

_____

_____

_____

Activation: What do you need from yourself and others to make the change?

_____

_____

_____

_____

_____

_____

Affirmation: What new thinking will you employ? Write your own encouragement to yourself. What is your affirmation?

_____

_____

_____

DAY 14: ACTION

What thinking and behaviors will you:

KEEP doing:

_____

_____

_____

_____

_____

_____

STOP doing:

_____

_____

_____

START doing:

_____

_____

_____

_____

_____

NOTES:

_____

_____

_____

WEEK THREE:

RE-PAIR & RE-NEW

Reflect for a moment; I'd like you to get an image of something in your head. What is something you own? You absolutely love it. Do you do maintenance and upkeep so meticulously that the object is considered immaculately maintained? Do you lavish it with so much care that someone may say you idolize it? Some may even say that you worship it. Now give yourself time to think pensively to get that image in your head. Close your eyes if that helps.

Pause reading.

Next, take that image of that thing and replace it with YOU. Do you give yourself as many repairs as you give to that thing? Well, this week, you will repair from the past and renew your relationships and yourself. This section is designed to help you take responsibility and forgive yourself for any role you've played in sabotaging your future, family, career, dreams, and possibly that of others. This week you reemerge with a higher version of yourself.

This week you will rejoice in letting go and moving towards your purpose with poise and unambiguous promise. Let's go to work!

DAY 15: WISDOM GUIDE #11

DO SOMETHING GOOD FOR SOMEONE
& DON'T TELL ANYONE

Acceptance:

Doing good for someone is subjective. First, what is good in the context of this wisdom? Good refers to the actions you take to impact others positively. Now, ask yourself, when I do good for others, am I practicing the Golden Rule or the Platinum Rule?

For this following explanation, I need you to apply the Q-TIP concept. This idea comes from my dear mentor and friend, Yvonne Robinson, which stands for "quit taking it personally." If you are using the Golden Rule as your guide to do for others, I'd like to offer up a mind shift.

The Golden Rule: actually focuses on what you want the other person to have.

The Platinum Rule: addresses what the other person wants for themselves.

I am a gift giver; it's my top love language. And I am never short of ideas of what I want other people to have. I've learned giving people a say in what you do for them makes for a more meaningful outcome. Instead of assuming that other stressed-out single moms would want a spa day, I had to give up my wanting to surprise them and, instead, have a conversation where they get to be a part of what I give them. For the sole purpose of teaching how to do something good for someone, I must share an example. Yes, after I just suggested to NOT tell anybody. SMH.

I recently wanted to support a mentee, colleague, and friend who is a single dad of three beautiful little ones. He was vulnerable to sharing his struggles, and immediately, I wanted to practice the Golden Rule and plan to have his little ones taken care of by a trusted friend, Uber him to the spa and back. Sounds fabulous to me, right? Because that's what I would appreciate at this moment.

Instead, I practiced the Platinum Rule and asked him what brings him absolute joy that he has not given to himself in a while. He responded, "live music and dancing." So off my radar for him. See, I have just deepened our relationship by finding out his desires. This approach helps me make my offer to support him through a challenging time. Now that I am aware, I asked him if he would like to look up the kinds of music he'd like and where, and I would take care of the rest, including childcare. There were tears on both sides. From his own voice, he acknowledged his gratefulness for being seen and supported. He also welcomed my invitation to be taken care of and the positive impact he felt. To be clear, I am not saying that one Rule is better than the other. I will, however, ask you to think about the end result.

Now you have added a tool to your arsenal to have healthy and meaningful relationships.

I witnessed my father mentor and model this lesson. Even though I grew up in a loving and supportive home with both my parents, four siblings, and anywhere from one to five other relatives at any given time, resources and money were tight. However, our financial circumstances did not hinder my father from giving his time and talent to others. My father rarely tells anyone. It was mostly because, Big Red (my mom) would be against him giving away what we didn't have. The recipients shared and told of his goodness. That taught me I did not have to bring up, boast or brag about what I do for others. If you genuinely give from an open heart, your good deeds will come to the public light through the people impacted.

Acknowledge: When you give to others do you tell anyone? What satisfaction or need does sharing what you do for others fulfill?

_____

_____

_____

_____

_____

_____

Application: What if you practiced this concept, how would your life, family, and career be different?

_____

_____

_____

_____

_____

Activation: What words, symbols, analogies, icons, memes will you use to shift your thinking and behavior in the future?

_____

_____

_____

_____

_____

Affirmation: I will give with an open heart without expectation or reciprocity. When I do good for others, I implicitly do good to and for myself. Today, I will make someone's day, and I won't tell anyone.

DAY 16: WISDOM GUIDE # 12

HONEST FEEDBACK IS A GIFT;
RECEIVING IT IS A BLESSING

Acceptance:

My clients, family, and friends often praise me for having all the right words to say when. Well, the truth is I've made an abundance of mistakes, and I take responsibility for most of them. I say "most" because clear and effective communication is hard. Therefore, if there was a miscommunication, all parties should own a part.

All that to say, because of my personality, I am not one to call people out. I tend to own what part was mine and not bring it up again. That is hard. But holding silence in those moments, even when the responsibility should have been shared, taught me this lesson.

Receiving feedback with openness and suspending defensiveness allows you to accrue multiple perspectives that enhance our efficacy with important relationships.

I remember really struggling on a project that I was subcontracted to do by one of my mentors. I was not operating at my usual high level of follow-through, and that mentor I revere had to give me some tough feedback. His feedback was honest, yet gentle. I started to respond with a counter for everything. In his masterful way, he got me to pause. Then he simply said, "Phyllis, receive the feedback."

Because I knew he cared about me, I could slow down and listen to understand versus defend, and I grew in that moment. So can you. Receiving critical feedback is a skill. Have you developed yours?

Acknowledge: What areas in life are you not open to critical feedback? How is that working for you? How might being open to critical feedback accelerate your success in that area?

_____

_____

_____

_____

_____

_____

Application: Choose someone you trust and believe truly cares about you. Ask them to give you some critical feedback about anything that does not align with what they know your values to be. What could be different in your life, your family or your career as a result?

_____

_____

_____

_____

_____

_____

Activation: What words, symbols, analogies, icons, memes will you use to shift your thinking and behavior in the future?

_____

_____

_____

_____

_____

_____

Affirmation: I care about my impact. I long for honest yet gentle feed forward. Awareness is the first step to change myself to change the world.

DAY 17: WISDOM GUIDE #13

PROGRESS IS A PROCESS

Acceptance:

What is progress? If running a mile is your goal, stretching and running for two steps is progress. If learning a second language is your goal, purchasing learning software or asking a native speaker to support your learning is progress. You see, progress is not the end result. It is whatever advancements you make in your goal direction.

Often, there is a tendency to compare our movement to others. Remember, when you work for, and towards your purpose, you are only competing with yourself.

What is a process? It is a series of actions or steps taken to achieve a particular end.

Let's make the connection. Your steps must be a series of actions. You must take more than one step or action to see progress.

I don't know if you are anything like me, but I wanted to achieve progress yesterday. Then, I ask myself, "Self, what steps have you taken today to progress towards your goals?" I ask myself this question because I have learned that if you are not intentional and strategic, your one-off attempts will not reap the progress you desire.

About 20 years ago, I attended a certification program. I was blown away by the framework and the proven results. I set my intentions on being a training faculty member and getting mentoring from the intercultural guru, Dr. Mitch Hammer. The first step I took was the scariest one. I reached out to him and shared how the certification changed my life and that I would welcome the opportunity to join this internationally known training team. It is vital that you speak into the universe your desires.

After about a year, the invitation to support a limited project was offered. Of course, I said yes. I supported that format for about three years. My highly favorable evaluations led to the day of my dreams. I opened my email one day, and there it was. I remember the feeling of pride and joy being overwhelming. Guess what? I even surpassed my dream by being invited to the think tank, which resulted in a new certification program in which I was offered the opportunity to be one of a small group trainers internationally.

Make a commitment to yourself, and don't break it. See it through. Your rewards await you.

Acknowledge: What is your process for progress? Is that process working for you? how so?

_____

_____

_____

_____

_____

_____

Application: What area in your life do you want to make progress? What will be your process? How will you measure success?

_____

_____

_____

_____

_____

_____

Activation: What words, symbols, analogies, icons, memes will you use to shift your thinking and behavior in the future?

_____

_____

_____

_____

_____

_____

Affirmation: One step leads to another. My process matters. I will take a step today, tomorrow, and the next toward my goal. victory is mine.

DAY 18: WISDOM GUIDE #14

WHAT EVIDENCE DO YOU HAVE
THAT YOU ARE NOT WORTHY

Acceptance:

The biggest lie about who we are is the one we tell ourselves. In the field of psychology, there is a talk therapy method called CBT. Cognitive behavioral therapy (CBT) is a structured, goal-oriented type of talk therapy. It can help manage mental health conditions, such as depression and anxiety, and emotional concerns, such as coping with grief or stress. It starts with a distressing situation/trigger →, which causes a person to have negative thoughts →, which causes negative emotions and physical distress → which leads to negative behaviors.

Examples of CBT techniques might include:

(1) Exposing yourself to situations that cause anxiety, like going into a crowded public space or

(2) Journaling about your thoughts throughout the day and recording your feelings about your thoughts.

Each of us has value. So, what happened to those of us who struggle to feel worthy of goodness and a life well-lived? Well, it's because I have been doing my work to recover from trauma as a child, which leads me to share this point. Instead of asking:

"What's wrong with you?" Ask, "What happened to you?"

In fact, if you question your success, ask yourself what evidence you have that you are not worthy. As you learned above, those negative thoughts will ride you on autopilot. I intentionally have to say to myself, "Phyllis, get off the crazy horse." It's a concept and wise guide I got from The Secret. It means that when you come into awareness of how your negative thoughts keep you on a hamster wheel, you acknowledge it and the impact of continuing to go down that path. Then you do something courageous – you interrupt that behavior by calculating how much evidence you have that makes your nuisance narrative trustworthy.

When I get that dream client, my negative thoughts try to overcome me. Remember, I am a work in progress. I will not lie. I still entertain those thoughts. When I do, and I am my highest self, I say out loud to myself, "Phyllis, get off the crazy horse." There's something about saying it out loud that connects with my innermost core, which is confident. Next, I try to find evidence that I don't deserve that dream client. I have been on the front lines of DEI work for over 25 years. And I'm damn good at it! I sent out an email to 100 people 17 years ago and haven't promoted for work since that day. I have a Bachelor's degree and two Master's degrees and am working on my Ed.D. During Covid, my business was nimble, adaptable, and agile. I quickly recreated all my in-person training to be online. My business grew over 300% during Covid when many small businesses and entrepreneurs didn't survive.

When I got the call from the world-renowned Miraval Resort & Spa to be their first Black female Thought Leader, I bawled like a baby. It was surreal for months. So much so I never publicly shared that I had been chosen. I felt that the opportunity would be withdrawn at any moment because I wasn't good enough, or not there yet, hadn't written a book, or had a Ph.D. They chose me because I was good enough right where I was. Oh, believe me, I put in the work. This opportunity did not happen overnight.

I had been going to that resort for about 15 years, and if I'm being honest, 15 years ago, my bestie, Allison, and I were the only Black bodies there. I stood out to them, which often is the case. Given my life choices, specifically about my education, I have been afforded rare opportunities to be in places of privilege with the privileged. Therefore, I am often the only one (person of color). You better believe I leverage those moments. So, who doesn't deserve to have their dream client seek them out? Well, I deserve it! I am worthy of success, and so are you.

Ladies if you need to get back in touch with yourself, I'm inviting your to join me at my women's retreat at Miraval. Holla at your girl (Https://thewholesouleexperience.com).

Acknowledge: Recall an area of your life that causes you to question why or how you got in such a good position, or was offered an awesome opportunity? Have you tried naming the evidence as to why? How did that work out for you, and if you haven't how's that working out for you?

_____

_____

_____

_____

_____

Application: If you are willing and able, try to think of other patterns of behavior that are associated with that unworthiness thinking. How could naming your evidence that you are worthy change your life, family, or career?

_____

_____

_____

_____

_____

Activation: What words, symbols, analogies, icons, and memes will you use to shift your thinking and behavior in the future?

_____

_____

_____

_____

_____

Affirmation: How and what I think about myself is critical to my success. I have the evidence. I am worthy – right now! I deserve success – right now!

DAY 19: WISDOM GUIDE #15

DANCE LIKE EVERYONE'S WATCHING
AND DANCE YOUR ASS OFF

Acceptance:

I love to dance. I have since I was a small child. And I'm pretty freaking good at it. Now, I am referring to dancing very literally as an art form. I teach urban soul line dancing, and now you know I am a competitive ballroom dancer. What I'd like you to do is to imagine your area of expertise as a dance. Dance in this story will be the metaphor for your "thing" – whatever that is. So, pause here, grab your "thing" out of its literal context, and use that "thing" to fill in your own story alongside mine.

When other folks are engaging with you and your dance, how confident are you? You've probably heard the phrase, "fake it til you make it." Well, that's different from what I'm talking about here. I'm talking about that "thing" you kick a$$ at doing. I mean, you love it, you light up when you do it, it energizes you, it's like a high when you do it, and seeing how your dance impacts others fortifies and renews your strength and confidence to do it again, and again, and again.

So, you may ask, "What's the wisdom in that, Phyllis?" I'm glad you asked. When that nuisance narrative enters your psyche, you must do the very thing nuisance narratives tell you not to do. And that, my friends, is the only way through it to keep some of your sanity. I believe that is the definition of courage I subscribe to sum it up. Be afraid – and do it anyway. Like I did during a training session with police officers.

This Wisdom Guide component connects to Wisdom Guide number #14 in that you may still need to accept your calling. Maybe that dance that you do really is that good. I would even venture to say your dance is off the chain, and it's hot, it's da shit [all old school language I grew up with, and I would also say that language is cultural].

See what had happened was I had an in-person training with over 100 Police Officers in a that was connected to a serious racialized incident. I live with general anxiety while still knowing I am "the bomb" at what I do. I can overcome my nuisance narrative more often than not in my professional world. But for some reason, my anxiety was exceptionally high to work with this group, especially in person. I was very attuned to my body and my mind. As soon as that imposter's voice and fear came in, I immediately spoke into existence what I wanted to feel like at that moment. And what I wanted my interactions with the group to be like versus not.

Throughout that five hours, I had to consistently speak positively to myself and continuously ask myself what evidence I had that the group didn't want to learn from a Black woman, would be defensive and disrespectful, would be hostile, would not willingly participate (fill in the blank with your own nuisance narrative). While all those negative thoughts were coming in, I drowned them out with:

"Phyllis, anyone who gets to engage with you is blessed and will leave a better person; Phyllis, you have a unique experience with police -use it" (and I did).

I continued, "Phyllis, you are so wicked smart, empathetic, funny, quick-witted, knowledgeable, and flawless looking -use it," and I did.

I continued, "Phyllis, everyone in this room is a great human with joy and love in their hearts."

Wow! Just pause and feel the lightness of that new narrative.

At the end of the session, the city's head of training and development was on the verge of tears when they handed me the evaluations. My training overall was rated above average and exceeded expectations at 96%, and 100% exceeded expectations for my expertise and delivery. I did it! I really did it with my PINK Partner in equity and inclusion, Tracy Duran. She was an anchor in that room for me. You may ask, "What is the wisdom in that, Phyllis?" Thanks for asking. You cannot excel to the top of your industry, class, or purpose alone. You need dance partners.

When I'm going into my arena, I'm taking a veteran DEI partner who's BETTER than me in with me. A compatible dance partner who balances your energy and your flaws. Success doesn't have to be about ego – it should be about impact. When you have the divine right partners, you can dance your ass off. And that's what WE did!

Acknowledge: Have you found your dance partner for that "thing" you're great at? How is having (or not having) one working for you? What qualities does your dance partner(s) have or you would want them to have?

_____

_____

_____

_____

_____

Application: If you have dance partner(s) already, how can you better leverage and strengthen the relational glue? If you have not been successful in attracting, yes, attracting your partner, think deeply and share how your life, family, and career would be different?

_____

_____

_____

_____

_____

Activation: What words, symbols, analogies, icons, memes will you use to shift your thinking and behavior in the future?

_____

_____

_____

_____

_____

_____

Affirmation: I am the divine right person for this dance and this moment; therefore, I cannot fail. I have (or will have) the divine right person show up in the arena with me. With them – I will not fail.

DAY 20: REFLECTION

Acknowledge: What highlights or insights did you gain?

_____

_____

_____

_____

_____

_____

Application: What is one concrete thing you can do differently?

_____

_____

_____

Activation: What do you need from yourself and others to make the change?

_____

_____

_____

_____

_____

Affirmation: What new thinking will you employ? Write your own encouragement to yourself. What is your affirmation?

_____

_____

_____

DAY 21: ACTION

What thinking and behaviors will you:

KEEP doing:

_____

_____

_____

_____

_____

_____

STOP doing:

_____

_____

_____

START doing:

_____

_____

_____

_____

_____

_____

NOTES:

_____

_____

_____

WEEK FOUR:
RE-START & RE-SULTS

Drivers, rev up our engines. It's time to restart your life and relationships to get better results. It's week four, and you've hung in there like a champ. Now that you have gotten clear on your purpose, you've renovated some negative thoughts and behaviors out of your life. Now, you're thinking about repairing yourself or your meaningful relationships. It is now time to trust and believe in your power. Light will overcome darkness every day of the week. It's time for you to turn on your light. For some, maybe they are still discovering what their light is. Some know, but do not let it shine; some already have a shine, but you can shine brighter.

You will gather there is no such thing as a small thing when you are moving in the direction of your dreams and being guided by your values. Remember those mistakes you dealt with in week two? It is time to use learning from those experiences that we don't even know have shaped us in some way.

Time out for playing small to keep others comfortable. Go ahead and let your light shine. If those around you are intimidated, that's theirs to hold, not you. But remain gentle and treat people so they can preserve their dignity even when that might be difficult. After you finish this week, you will be ready to fight for your dreams with an arsenal of love, empathy, and compassion. I believe, as my colleague and mentor Beth would say, "be soft on people and hard on systems." Time out for beating yourself up about your past. Time in for being fully present, this day, and showing up for yourself in a way you have never done before.

It is time to get results in your life. You picked up this journal, and that was a great start. Hang in here with me for this last week. You will be untouchable if you practice these wisdom guides and the ones you are creating along the way.

This section is the last week – make it count!

DAY 22: WISDOM GUIDE #16

TRUST AND BELIEVE YOUR POWER

Acceptance:

Did you know you have power? Yes, you have personal power over yourself and your mind. As a person with diagnosed anxiety and other mental health challenges, I practice many mind-over-matter strategies. Those nuisance narratives will get the best of you every time if you do not fight back with positive narratives that feed your spirit.

For me, "trust" means relying on something or someone without evidence or investigation. And believe means that I am assured without a doubt.

I learned this wisdom at Miraval Resort & Spa during an equine experience. The goal was to get my horse, Imus, to lift its foot so I could clean the hay from around its shoe. Now, you need to know that I had an extreme fear of animals at this time in my life. And I find myself standing beside a nearly one-ton horse. Another important thing you should also know is that horses are prey animals. When animals in the wild are prey, they are super sensitive to the energy around them.

After the facilitators demonstrated the task and some safety education, we were instructed to take a turn. The instructions were to walk up to the horse on one side (not from the front) with your full intention and attention on the horse and the goal. Easier said than done.

Let me paint this picture for you. If I'm scared as hell, but the horse doesn't know why. Therefore, Imus will take his cue from my energy to determine if he is safe. Given that I could not harness my fear, I could not get Imus to lift his foot. You may ask, "Why Phyllis?" It was because I didn't trust or believe that I could. To be fully transparent, if it were not for my best friend making fun of my failure, I would not have tried as many times as I did.

Fast forward ten years later, I returned to this equine experience with a vengeance. Remember, I am a competitive person. I had to know and prove I could do it – for myself. This time, I embodied the mindset that was instructed for me to be successful. I knew I could be super focused. I suppressed my fear to get the horse to stay calm enough for me to pinch the appropriate nerves connected to the foot to get Imus to lift it. I got my mind right and walked toward Imus with a strong energy that communicated that I was calm and in charge. And I did it! I trusted, and it worked because I knew it was possible. I believed I could do it because I knew I could accomplish anything I put my mind, energy, and actions toward achieving. Remember your superpower – your energy, thoughts, and actions you bring to any situation can change the atmosphere and outcome.

Acknowledge: Can you recall a time when you trusted something, but didn't believe it? Can you tell the difference?

_____

_____

_____

_____

_____

_____

Application: Visual an outcome you want for yourself. What energy and action would you bring to that goal if you trusted AND believed it could happen for you? How could shifting your energy and actions change your life, family, or career?

_____

_____

_____

_____

_____

_____

Activation: What words, symbols, analogies, icons, and memes will you use to shift your thinking and behavior in the future?

_____

_____

_____

_____

_____

Affirmation: I am the one I've been waiting for. I trust and believe with all my heart and soul that I am capable. I am the one I've been waiting for.

DAY 23: WISDOM GUIDE #17

NO SUCH THING AS A SMALL THING

Acceptance:

One of my mentors constantly reminds me that small things lead to big things. Therefore, any action you take to uplift humanity is a big thing. So, I've learned to do the small things with grandeur. It's like using a mindset to under promise and over-deliver.

It sounds like a small thing, right?

Try this on. I have already established in this journal that I am not a fan of social media. However, I cognitively know I must stay technologically literate. My fingers are just procrastinating. Seriously though, I made myself go on LinkedIn one day at my workday midpoint.

The workday midpoint for me is between 5–6 pm (with an 7:30 am start). I try to peel myself from my office chair and at least feed my body and brain before I start back up around 6–7 pm to respond to emails, voicemails, website inquires, grad class, homework, write proposals, invoice clients, prep for the next day's training or keynote with about a 2–3 am shutdown time if I'm lucky. Yes, you read it right [every day a sistah husslin]. More about my poor self-care later.

Back to the story, see, what had happened was I jumped on LinkedIn with disdain in my heart. Yet, immediately upon logging on, I received a message from a highly recognizable international female-focused company that had attended one of my public DEI trainings. I paused and did a happy dance, then I responded with intention. I immediately informed her I wasn't on LinkedIn as much as I should have, and her inquiry was a high priority and asked if she would continue the conversation through text message. Funny, someone will pick up this journal years from now and must look up what a text message was. Hahaha. She messaged me her number, and I texted her back immediately. I inquired about her time and willingness to jump on Zoom to have a conversation.

She was impressed that I promptly made myself available to her with a sense of urgency, and I was willing to share my personal cell number with her as the CEO of the company. Long story short, I nailed it and got a next-step meeting to partner before we got off that Zoom call. Fast forward, in less than two weeks, they chose to go with the biggest ticket item I had proposed, and we started the procurement process.

One might say, "Phyllis, that was just doing what you should be doing." Slow your roll. I do not open my email or voicemail. It gives me great anxiety—more about that in this journal. My team captures what I need to respond to, and it can take up to 3 months to get an initial meeting with me. Yes, I am that chick in the DEI world.

The potential client knew from the training she attended that I was in high demand, so imagine what my personal touch did as the CEO and Founder. Now, to be fully transparent, the contract was small, but wow, it did have big potential. Mainly because the work would be individually customized for the C-Suite, and they have decision-making power and budgets across the entire company.

You should also know that this company has been on my dream list for over 30 years. You should also know that just a week before this meeting, I accomplished a 30-year dream of starting a nonprofit focused on women and girls, wholeSOUL, Inc. Therefore, the company was not on my dream list as a client; they were on my list to partner with my nonprofit. Now, from that small act, I can potentially have them as both a client and partner with my nonprofit. I'm getting my "shout on" just thinking about it. So, do I need to repeat it? There's no such thing as a small thing.

Acknowledge: What is one small step you can take today towards something big that you really want? How has taking a step towards something bigger worked out for you in the past?

_____

_____

_____

_____

_____

_____

Application: Think of a dream you have, reframe your mindset and outlook that there are no small things when you are moving towards goodness. How would life, family and your career be different?

_____

_____

_____

_____

_____

_____

Activation: What words, symbols, analogies, icons, memes will you use to shift your thinking and behavior in the future?

_____

_____

_____

_____

_____

_____

Affirmation: I am not a small thing. I am a force; therefore, whatever step I take in the direction of good will manifest in a big thing.

DAY 24: WISDOM GUIDE #18

PLAYING SMALL TO KEEP OTHER PEOPLE COMFORTABLE STUNTS YOUR GROWTH

Acceptance:

Oh, this was a hard one for me. When I turned 50, it was like a switch flipped in me. I didn't realize how much energy I spent keeping other people comfortable. Because, low and behold, if anyone were to have a problem with me, it was an issue. For the record, I hate conflict. I know hate is a strong word. I mean this strongly. I absolutely despise conflict. Conflict makes me feel like ants are crawling all over my body. How about that for a visual? It's ironic that I manage conflict for a living. I literally facilitate a lot of conflict on the interpersonal, group, and organizational level, daily at work and in my personal life. So, facilitating conflict is a far better position to be in than being one involved in the conflict.

What I learned about myself is that when I highly respect someone, I tend to dim my light. Why do I do that? Some of it is cultural, and some facets remain in question. I've shared that I work in the field of DEI (diversity, equity, and inclusion). I would co-facilitate with my mentors for much of my tenure in the industry. While I may have looked like a swan on the surface, I was a foot-flapping sistah, trying to hold my head above water underneath.

You should also know I come from a culture of authoritarians where reverence is expected. Meaning my parents were no joke on discipline, nor did they permit input on decisions. You don't question, and you like it regardless.

Somehow, growing up with those messages shows up in me not speaking truth to power when titles and tenure are present. I have been acculturated to minimize myself when the other party has a "title," or they are "older."

The wisdom I've come to is that when you hold another human being in a regard higher than yourself, you will not be yourself – your whole self. This mindset was the truth in every aspect of my life until I turned 50. I refuse to cower now. While your title is important and should be respected, so does mine. I have tenure and am more seasoned due to my lived experiences. So why in the heck am I playing small like I'm not as knowledgeable, experienced, or confident as anyone else?

No one is better than me or less. We are equally complex humans, and each has a divine purpose on this earth. Each of us has gifts, but only some get access and the opportunity to share those gifts with the world.

It's staggering that the number of people around you can tell you how brilliant and great you are. Still, you will only be able to reach your highest height once you believe it and trust it for yourself. Have you seen you when you believe and trust in yourself? You are something fascinating to watch.

Acknowledge: What areas in your life do you play small or minimize your whole self? How is that working for you?

_____

_____

_____

_____

_____

_____

Application: Let's focus on one area you identified above. If you were to show up in your light and brilliance, how might life be different for you, your family, your career?

_____

_____

_____

_____

_____

_____

Activation: What words, symbols, analogies, icons, memes will you use to shift your thinking and behavior in the future?

_____

_____

_____

_____

_____

_____

Affirmation: I am a whole person. I will bring my whole self forward. If I cannot, I must move away from that relationship and move forward with myself and others that long for the real me to show up.

DAY 25: WISDOM GUIDE #19

FIGHT FOR YOUR DREAMS
LIKE YOUR LIFE DEPENDS ON IT

Acceptance:

What are your dreams for your life, your family, and your career? A dream is to contemplate the possibility of doing something. Dreams can be big and small. I have multiple dreams and have been blessed to dream bigger ones. How many people get to say that? Well, fewer than you think, but that can be different for you. If you are wondering how to get started, this section is just for you.

Well, first, you actually have to dream. What are your most deeply held values, and how do you want to see them manifested in the world – to do good?

Some of my dreams were small, and they were also self-centered. However, in my early twenties, I realized that even though my dreams were about my own aspirations and successes, those individual accomplishments allowed me to dream bigger dreams that impact the world.

That realization created a "fight" in me that is undying, unmovable, unshakeable, and relentless. Did you know "relentless" means - oppressively constant?

If you don't think you have a dream in you, ask yourself, "what occupies your mental, spiritual, and psychological space – constantly"? Name that thing, so you can hunt it down and capture it like it was only meant for you.

About 12 years ago, I was introduced to a ballroom dance called Chicago 8 Count Stepping. I fell in love at first sight. I wanted to not only learn the dance but master it. So I surrounded myself with the best Steppers around the world. I was the epitome of relentless. I took group, private, out-of-town, and intra-town lessons and danced every weekend and many weekdays. Within one year, I started competing. Within three years, I had won 3 titles, with my biggest accomplishment playing out on the Chicago Steppin' World's Largest Competition stage. Talk about the fight – just having the courage to get on the stage after only two and half years of dancing with couples from around the world who had been doing it ten-plus years longer.

If you don't have a dream for yourself, I strongly encourage you to do so. There is no greater reward than to prove to yourself you can do it. I dare you. Just dream one dream for yourself and act on it as your life depends on it. I have no doubt you will acquire success in some form or fashion. That success will propel you to your next dream. Before you know it, you have dreamed a bigger dream that eventually touches and impacts humanity beyond your wildest imagination. If you have a dream that doesn't scare you, you're not dreaming big enough.

Acknowledge: What is one thing you have fought for with all your might? How did that work out for you? Did you experience success?

_____

_____

_____

_____

_____

_____

Application: What is one thing in your life right now that means everything to you? What can you do more of to achieve success?

_____

_____

_____

_____

_____

_____

Activation: What words, symbols, analogies, icons, memes will you use to shift your thinking and behavior in the future?

_____

_____

_____

_____

_____

_____

Affirmation: My dreams have meaning beyond me. The world is waiting on me.

DAY 26: WISDOM GUIDE #20

IS YOUR GOAL TO BE RIGHT OR BE EFFECTIVE?

Acceptance:
   When I am my highest self in challenging situations, I pause and ask myself, "In this moment, what is your goal – to be right or to get results?"

Now, let's look at both concepts.
What is a goal?
It is the result or outcome you want.

What does it mean to be right or be effective?
Being right means, I respond to be heard.
Being effective means I respond to be understood.

   When you approach your most meaningful relationships with intentions of the best possible outcomes, you've already won. That's right! While this framing may be simple, giving yourself permission to slow down in difficult interactions is not easy. Being right is vital to support our ego and confidence. However, your end results will vary when being right is only about our ego rather than the human connection.
   Effectiveness starts with a conscious choice to a commitment to starting with the end in mind. Being right can give you a momentary surge of one-upmanship. However, there is no greater lasting feeling that replays authentic joy than being effective. In my experience, feelings associated with being right usually fade quickly from triumph to feeling terrible about the state of the relationship you just blew up. "Message" (in my Damon Wayans voice)! Focus on getting it right than being right.

Acknowledge: Do you tend to be a person who wants to be right? How is that working for you?

_____

_____

_____

_____

_____

_____

Application: Think about an event or situation you are facing where you can focus on your goal and the outcome you want, how might your end results be different?

_____

_____

_____

_____

_____

_____

Activation: What words, symbols, analogies, icons, memes will you use to shift your thinking and behavior in the future?

_____

_____

_____

_____

_____

_____

Affirmation: I will start with the end result in mind. I will allow myself to pause and be fully present. When I am effective, ultimately, I am not only right, but I deepened my human connection with others.

DAY 27: REFLECTION

Acknowledge: What highlights or insights did you gain?

_____

_____

_____

_____

_____

_____

Application: What is one concrete thing you can do differently?

_____

_____

_____

Activation: What do you need from yourself and others to make the change?

_____

_____

_____

_____

_____

Affirmation: What new thinking will you employ? Write your own encouragement to yourself. What is your affirmation?

_____

_____

_____

DAY 28: ACTION

What thinking and behaviors will you:

KEEP doing:

_____

_____

_____

_____

_____

_____

STOP doing:

_____

_____

_____

START doing:

_____

_____

_____

_____

_____

_____

NOTES:

_____

_____

_____

DAY 29: REFLECTING ON YOUR
NEW INTENTIONS

Where did you find success from your 30 day journey?

_____

_____

_____

_____

_____

This journey allowed me to:

_____

_____

_____

_____

_____

What barriers got in the way of your journey?

_____

_____

_____

_____

What solutions did you create?

_____

_____

_____

_____

_____

DAY 30: ACTING ON YOUR
NEW INTENTIONS

30 days from today, I will...

_____

_____

_____

_____

_____

60 days from today, I will...

_____

_____

_____

_____

_____

90 days from today, I will...

_____

_____

_____

_____

_____

365 days from today, I will...

_____

_____

_____

_____

_____

ABOUT THE AUTHOR:
PHYLLIS D. BRAXTON

Phyllis D. Braxton is a mother, wife, author, artist, interculturalist, and a world-renown Miraval Thought Leader bridging theory and practice in the DEI and self-care space. Phyllis has over 25 years of international touchpoints with tens of thousands of people with experience in trauma-informed diversity, equity and inclusion training and facilitation, leadership coaching, conflict communication, intercultural competence, organizational development, and clinical therapy. Phyllis received her Bachelor's degree from Morris Brown College in Atlanta, Ga., a Master's of Adult Education from the University of MN, and a Master of Clinical Social Work from St. Catherine's University.

Phyllis was an adjunct professor, and has studied diversity and cultural trends from around the world. Her reach extends abroad from the US Shores—from Iceland to Dubai, and even the deep south to the West Coast. She helps others leverage their identities and experiences to foster healthy relationships for more inclusive workplace outcomes and homelife satisfaction. A self-described "edutainer" and "intellectual activist," she believes in meeting people where they are without blame, shame, or judgment.

Through laughter and human connection, Phyllis continues encouraging people to examine their life experiences and practice key life lessons with humor and grace. As a lifelong learner, Phyllis is currently a doctoral student studying Leadership for Change specializing in Evidence-Based Coaching.

She was born and raised in Moss Point, MS. She now resides in Minneapolis, Minnesota. And she is determined to leave a legacy of generational transformation for racially, economically, and educationally disadvantaged women and girls through her non-profit, wholeSOUL, Inc. Pursuing Intercultural Needs & Knowledge (PINK) Consulting, LLC provides the above areas of expertise for individuals, teams, and organizations globally. Phyllis brings shine and leaves light wherever she goes.

Learn more about Phyllis at:
PinkConsultingLLC.com
PhyllisBraxton.com
wholesoulinc.org
phyllisitate.com

Follow Phyllis on Social Media:
Facebook: https://www.facebook.com/phyllis.braxton.54
Instagram: https://www.instagram.com/pinkconsulting/
Linkedin: https://www.linkedin.com/in/phyllisdbraxton
YouTube: https://www.youtube.com/user/pbraxton1908

Made in the USA
Coppell, TX
25 September 2023

22017837R10063